Baby's First Year

BY
MARCIA O. LEVIN

CRESCENT BOOKS

NEW YORK

ILLUSTRATIONS

Mary Cassatt
BABY CHARLES LOOKING OVER HIS MOTHER'S
SHOULDER (No. 3)
c. 1900
oil on canvas
27⅛ × 20⅜"
Collection: The Brooklyn Museum; Carl H. DeSilver Fund

Pablo Picasso
MOTHER AND CHILD
1921
oil on canvas
56½ × 64"
The Art Institute of Chicago
© S.P.A.D.E.M., Paris/V.A.G.A., New York 1984

Berthe-Marie-Pauline Morisot
THE CRADLE
1873
oil on canvas
21½ × 18"
The Louvre, Paris
Courtesy: Service de Documentation Photographique de la
Réunion des Musées Nationaux, Paris

Mary Cassatt
MATERNAL CARESS
1891
color print with drypoint, soft-ground, and aquatint
14⅜ × 10½"
National Gallery of Art, Washington, D.C.; Gift of Miss
Elisabeth Achelis 1942

Mary Cassatt
BABY REACHING FOR AN APPLE
1893
oil on canvas
39½ × 25¾"
Virginia Museum of Fine Arts, Richmond; Gift of Anonymous
Donor 1975

Milton Avery
MOTHER AND CHILD
1944
oil on canvas
40 × 30"
Private Collection, Courtesy: Andrew Crispo Gallery, Inc., New
York

Grandma Moses
ROCKABYE
1957
oil on masonite
11⅞ × 16"
Private Collection
Copyright © 1973, Grandma Moses Properties Co., New York.

Calligraphy by *Calligraphy Studios*
NEW YORK

Cover fabric: The Framingham Hearts Delite Collection.
Copyright © Wamsutta/O.T.C. Courtesy of Wamsutta/O.T.C.,
a division of Springs Industries, Inc.

This 1994 edition is published by Crescent Books,
distributed by Random House Value Publishing Inc.,
40 Engelhard Avenue, Avenel, New Jersey 07001.

Printed in China

ISBN 0-517-07010-3

8 7 6 5 4

Mary Cassatt
LITTLE ANN SUCKING HER FINGER, EMBRACED BY HER
MOTHER
1897
pastel on beige paper
21¾ × 17"
Collection: Jeu de Paume Museum, Paris
Courtesy: Service de Documentation Photographique de la Réunion
des Musées Nationaux, Paris

Mary Cassatt
BABY'S FIRST CARESS
1891
pastel on paper
30 × 24"
New Britain Museum of American Art, Connecticut; Harriett
Russell Stanley Fund

Auguste Renoir
GABRIELLE ET JEAN
oil on canvas
Grenoble Museum
Courtesy: Art Resource, New York

Mary Cassatt
BABY IN DARK BLUE SUIT
1889
oil on canvas
29 × 23½"
Cincinnati Art Museum; Gift of John J. Emery Endowment

Edmund Charles Tarbell
MOTHER AND CHILD IN A BOAT
1892
oil on canvas
30 × 35"
Museum of Fine Arts, Boston; Bequest of David B. Kimball
in memory of his wife, Clara Bertram Kimball.

Maurice Prendergast
LARGE BOSTON PUBLIC GARDEN SKETCHBOOK, page 29
Woman pushing a perambulator and talking to a little girl.
c. 1895−97
watercolor on paper
14¼ × 11¼"
The Metropolitan Museum of Art; Robert Lehman Collection, 1975.

Pablo Picasso
MOTHER AND CHILD
Dinard, Summer 1922
oil on canvas
39½ × 31½"
The Baltimore Museum of Art; The Cone Collection, formed
by Dr. Claribel Cone and Miss Etta Cone of Baltimore, Maryland.
© S.P.A.D.E.M., Paris/V.A.G.A., New York 1984

Dedication

This book tells what happened
from the day you were born until
you were one year old.

Some day you will be able to
read about these things by yourself.

And in a few years, years that
will pass very slowly for you, but very
quickly for us, perhaps you will show
this book to a child of your own.

BABY CHARLES LOOKING OVER HIS MOTHER'S SHOULDER—Mary Cassatt

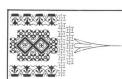

This book belongs to

_____

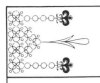

You Arrive

Monday's child is fair of face
Tuesday's child is full of grace
Wednesday's child is full of woe
Thursday's child has far to go
Friday's child is loving and giving
Saturday's child works hard for a living
But the child who is born on the Sabbath day
Is bonny and blithe, and good and gay.

When

_____
Day of the week   Hour   Month   Day   Year

Where

_____
Place

_____
Address

Who Helped To Deliver You

Name _____

Address _____

Signature _____

Name _____

Address _____

Signature _____

Name _____

Address _____

Signature _____

Name _____

Address _____

Signature _____

7

Your Name

First _____

Middle _____

Last _____

Your name was chosen by

_____

You were given your name because

_____

Your name means

_____

Your Handprint   *Your Footprint*

MOTHER AND CHILD—*Pablo Picasso*

Birth Information

Color of hair _____

Color of eyes _____

Weight _____

Length _____

Identifying marks _____

Your First Picture

Paste Photo Here

Date _____

Taken at _____

The First Time We Saw You

Mother said

_____

_____

_____

_____

Father said

_____

_____

_____

_____

THE CRADLE—Berthe-Marie-Pauline Morisot

Your Birth Certificate

Paste
Birth Certificate
Here

Paste
Birth Announcement
Here

Your Horoscope

The day you were born

Paste
Horoscope
Here

Printed in _____

Your zodiac sign _____

Your birthstone _____

MOTHER AND CHILD—*Milton Avery*

Headlines in the News

The day you were born

World events

_____

_____

_____

Local events

_____

_____

_____

Weather that day

_____

_____

What the World Was Like

President of the United States

_____

Vice-President of the United States

_____

Popular Songs

_____

Most popular films and plays

_____

Most popular actors and actresses

_____

Best-selling books

_____

Latest fad

_____

What women were wearing

_____

What men were wearing

_____

How people traveled

_____

Name of
Grandmother's Mother
(your great-grandma)

Name of
Grandmother's Father
(your great-grandpa)

Name of
Grandfather's Mother
(your great-grandma)

Name of
Grandfather's Father
(your great-grandpa)

Birth Date

Birth Date

Birth Date

Birth Date

Birth Place

Birth Place

Birth Place

Birth Place

Name of Mother's Mother
(your grandmother)

Name of Mother's Father
(your grandfather)

Birth Date

Birth Date

Birth Place

Birth Place

Mother's Full Name

Birth Date

Birth Place

BABY REACHING FOR AN APPLE—Mary Cassatt

Father's Family Tree

Name of Grandmother's Mother (your great-grandma)	Name of Grandmother's Father (your great-grandpa)	Name of Grandfather's Mother (your great-grandma)	Name of Grandfather's Father (your great-grandpa)
Birth Date	Birth Date	Birth Date	Birth Date
Birth Place	Birth Place	Birth Place	Birth Place

Name of Father's Mother (your grandmother)	Name of Father's Father (your grandfather)
Birth Date	Birth Date
Birth Place	Birth Place

Father's Full Name

Birth Date

Birth Place

Other Relatives

Name	How Related	Birth Date

How many miles to Baby-land?
Anyone can tell
Up one flight,
To your right;
Please to ring the bell.

Who is the Queen of Baby-land?
Mother kind and sweet;
And her love,
Born above,
Guides the little feet.

George Cooper

Gift   From

_____

_____

_____

_____

_____

24

MATERNAL CARESS—Mary Cassatt

Visitors

and what they said about you

Visitors

and what they said about you

Who Took Care of You

At the beginning

　　Name _____

　　Relationship _____

　　Your reaction _____

Who helped

　　Name _____

　　Relationship _____

　　Your reaction _____

As you got bigger

　　Name _____

　　Relationship _____

　　Name _____

　　Relationship _____

　　Name _____

　　Relationship _____

ROCKABYE—Grandma Moses

Where You First Lived

Street _____

City _____

State _____

When we moved there

_____

What you liked best about this place

_____

_____

_____

_____

Picture of the Place Where You Lived

Paste Photo Here

A Typical Day

6 A.M. _____   6 P.M. _____

7 A.M. _____   7 P.M. _____

8 A.M. _____   8 P.M. _____

9 A.M. _____   9 P.M. _____

10 A.M. _____   10 P.M. _____

11 A.M. _____   11 P.M. _____

12 Noon _____   12 Midnight _____

1 P.M. _____   1 A.M. _____

2 P.M. _____   2 A.M. _____

3 P.M. _____   3 A.M. _____

4 P.M. _____   4 A.M. _____

5 P.M. _____   5 A.M. _____

Medical Information

Doctor's Name _____

Address _____

Telephone _____

Dates of Visits   What the Doctor Said

_____   _____
                             _____
                             _____
_____   _____
                             _____
                             _____
_____   _____
                             _____
                             _____
_____   _____
                             _____
                             _____

Accidents and Illnesses

When I was sick and lay a-bed,
I had two pillows at my head,
And all my toys about me lay
To keep me happy all the day.
                    Robert Louis Stevenson

Date	What Happened	Treatment

Medical Record

Inoculations:	Dates	Dates of Boosters
DPT { Diptheria	_____	_____
Whooping Cough	_____	_____
Tetanus	_____	_____
Polio	_____	_____
Measles	_____	_____
Rubella	_____	_____
Rubeola	_____	_____
Other	_____	_____

Tests:	Dates	Results
Tuberculin	_____	_____
Others	_____	_____
Blood type	_____	_____
Allergies	_____	_____

Dental Record

Dental Chart

Central Incisor
at _____ months

Lateral Incisor
at _____ months

Cuspid
at _____ months

First Molar
at _____ months

First Molar
at _____ months

Cuspid
at _____ months

Lateral Incisor
at _____ months

Central Incisor
at _____ months

Upper

Lower

Central Incisor
at _____ months

Lateral Incisor
at _____ months

Cuspid
at _____ months

First Molar
at _____ months

First Molar
at _____ months

Cuspid
at _____ months

Lateral Incisor
at _____ months

Central Incisor
at _____ months

Teething Problems _____

_____

_____

LITTLE ANN SUCKING HER FINGER, EMBRACED BY HER MOTHER—Mary Cassatt

You Learned To Do So Many Things

Bye, baby bunting
Daddy's gone a-hunting.
To get a little rabbit skin
To wrap the baby bunting in.

What   When

   Lifted your head   _____

   Grasped someone's finger   _____

   Looked at things overhead   _____

   Rolled to one side   _____

   Recognized Mother or Dad   _____

Paste Photo Here

38

Brow brinkie,
Eye winkie,
Mouth merry,
Cheek Cherry,
Chin-chopper, chin-chopper,
Chin-chopper chin.

(Say this rhyme as you
    point to baby's features)

What   **When**

   Held your head steady   _____

   Rolled onto your tummy   _____

   Sat, propped up   _____

   Recognized people who
       took care of you   _____

Paste Photo Here

Ride a cock horse
To Banbury Cross,
To see a fine lady
Ride on a white horse.

What   When

Liked to bounce on
    someone's knee   _____

Reached for a toy   _____

Liked to bite   _____

Banged a toy on
    a table top   _____

Paste Photo Here

BABY'S FIRST CARESS—Mary Cassatt

"Where's the baby?"   "Here (s)he is!"

What	When
Played "Where's the baby?" (or "Peek-a-boo!")	_____
Recognized familiar faces	_____
Sat up by yourself	_____
Got up on your hands and knees	_____
Hit two blocks together	_____

Paste Photo Here

Pat-a-cake, pat-a-cake, baker's man,
Bake me a cake as fast as you can;
Pat it and prick it, and mark it with a B,
And put it in the oven for Baby and me.

What   When

    Played pat-a-cake   _____

    Began to crawl   _____

    Pulled yourself up with support   _____

    Piled one block on top of another   _____

    Threw things out of your
          highchair or bed   _____

Paste Photo Here

43

Hickory dickory dock;
The mouse ran up the clock.
The clock struck one;
The mouse ran down,
Hickory dickory dock.

What   When

    Enjoyed rhymes

    Walked with one hand held   _____

    Gave someone a toy when asked   _____

    Put beads into a box   _____

    Held out an arm when being dressed   _____

Paste Photo Here

44

GABRIELLE ET JEAN—*Auguste Renoir*

Now You Can Walk

Now you can go wherever you want
Wherever you want to go
One foot out and the other foot out
That's all you need to know.

Oscar Hammerstein
"Allegro"

Took your first step alone _____
When

Paste Photo Here

46

The Way You Grew

How big is the baby? Soooo big!

Age	Height	Weight
1 month		
2 months		
3 months		
4 months		
5 months		
6 months		
7 months		
8 months		
9 months		
10 months		
11 months		

At one year, you weighed _____

Your height was _____

The Way You Slept

Sleep, baby, sleep;
Thy father tends the sheep.
Thy mother tends the dreamland tree,
And from it fall sweet dreams for thee;
Sleep, baby, sleep.

When

You slept through one of the night feedings _____

You slept through the night _____

Your morning nap changed _____

Your favorite way to sleep was _____

_____

Your bedtime toys were _____

_____

Other comments _____

_____

_____

BABY IN DARK BLUE SUIT—Mary Cassatt

The Way You Ate

A child should always say what's true.
And speak when he is spoken to,
And behave mannerly at table:
At least so far as he is able.

Robert Louis Stevenson

What	When
You began to chew food	_____
You ate from a spoon and fork	_____
You drank from a cup	_____
You held your own spoon	_____
You held your own cup	_____
You drank by yourself	_____
You fed yourself	_____

Your first "real" food was _____

_____

The foods you liked best were _____

_____

The foods you liked least were _____

_____

Comments _____

_____

50

The Way You Talked

Happy talk, keep talking happy talk.
Talk about things you like to do.
You've got to have a dream
If you don't have a dream
How're you going to make a dream come true?

> Oscar Hammerstein
> "South Pacific"

What you did	When
Made cooing sounds	_____
Laughed	_____
Noticed voices	_____
Said mmmmmm	_____
Made other sounds	_____
Said Da-da	_____

When you were one year old,
  you could say _____

_____

_____

The Places You Visited

You, friendly Earth, how far do you go,
With wheat fields that nod and rivers that flow,
With cities, and gardens, and cliffs, and isles,
And people upon you for thousands of miles?

Matthew Browne

Your first trip outdoors was _____

_____

The ride you took most often was _____

_____

You liked to ride in _____

_____

Your favorite place to visit was _____

_____

_____

Your longest trip was _____

_____

_____

MOTHER AND CHILD IN A BOAT—*Edmund Charles Tarbell*

Your Favorite Things

Raindrops on roses and whiskers on kittens,
Bright copper kettles and warm woolen mittens,
Brown paper packages tied up with string
These are a few of my favorite things.

Oscar Hammerstein
"The Sound of Music"

Your favorite toys _____

_____

Your favorite games _____

_____

Your favorite rhymes _____

_____

Your favorite books _____

Your favorite animals _____

Your favorite people _____

_____

Your First Birthday

The weather that day _____

_____

Where you were _____

_____

What you wore _____

_____

Who was there _____

_____

_____

_____

What you did _____

_____

_____

How you acted _____

_____

_____

Your gifts _____

_____

_____

_____

_____

55

Your Schedule at One Year

A Typical Day

Morning

_____

_____

_____

_____

Afternoon

_____

_____

_____

_____

Evening

_____

_____

_____

_____

Night

_____

_____

_____

_____

WOMAN PUSHING A PERAMBULATOR AND TALKING TO A LITTLE GIRL—*Maurice Prendergast*

We'll Always Remember

Your reaction to _____
_____
_____

What you did when _____
_____
_____

What you said when _____
_____
_____

The funniest thing that happened
to you was _____
_____
_____
_____

The cutest thing you did was _____
_____
_____
_____
_____

And Most of All

We want you to remember that:

Every flutter of the wing,
Every note of song we sing,
Every murmur, every tone,
Is of love, and love alone.

Henry Wadsworth Longfellow

We will always love you as
much as we have loved you
during your first wonderful year.

Afterthoughts

Milestones, comments and memorable events
as you grew :

_____

_____

_____

_____

_____

_____

_____

_____

_____

_____

MOTHER AND CHILD—Pablo Picasso

Afterthoughts

Milestones, comments and memorable events
as you grew:

_____

_____

_____

_____

_____

_____

_____

_____

_____

_____

Afterthoughts

Milestones, comments and memorable events
as you grew :

_____

_____

_____

_____

_____

_____

_____

_____

_____

_____

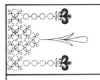

Afterthoughts

Milestones, comments and memorable events
as you grew:

_____

_____

_____

_____

_____

_____

_____

_____

_____

_____